📖 READERS

Pre-level 1

Fishy Tales
Colorful Days
Garden Friends
Party Fun
In the Park

Farm Animals
Petting Zoo
Let's Make Music
Cuentos de Peces *en español*
Dias Ilenos de color *en español*
Meet the Dinosaurs

Level 1

A Day at Greenhill Farm
Truck Trouble
Tale of a Tadpole
Surprise Puppy!
Duckling Days
A Day at Seagull Beach
Whatever the Weather
Busy Buzzy Bee
Big Machines
Wild Baby Animals
A Bed for the Winter
Born to be a Butterfly
Dinosaur's Day
Feeding Time
Diving Dolphin
Rockets and Spaceships
My Cat's Secret
First Day at Gymnastics
A Trip to the Zoo

I Can Swim!
A Trip to the Library
A Trip to the Doctor
LEGO: Trouble at the Bridge
LEGO: Secret at Dolphin Bay
Star Wars: What is a Wookiee?
A Day in the Life of a Builder
A Day in the Life of a Dancer
A Day in the Life of a Firefighter
A Day in the Life of a Teacher
A Day in the Life of a Musician
A Day in the Life of a Doctor
A Day in the Life of a Police Officer
A Day in the Life of a TV Reporter
Gigantes de Hierro *en español*
Crías del mundo animal *en español*
A Trip to the Dentist
Spider-Man: The Amazing Story
I Want To Be A Ballerina

Level 2

Dinosaur Dinners
Fire Fighter!
Bugs! Bugs! Bugs!
Slinky, Scaly Snakes!
Animal Hospital
The Little Ballerina
Munching, Crunching, Sniffing,
    and Snooping
The Secret Life of Trees
Winking, Blinking, Wiggling,
    and Waggling
Astronaut: Living in Space
Twisters!
Holiday! Celebration Days
    around the World
The Story of Pocahontas
Horse Show
Survivors: The Night the
    Titanic Sank
Eruption! The Story of Volcanoes

The Story of Columbus
Journey of a Humpback Whale
Amazing Buildings
Feathers, Flippers, and Feet
Outback Adventure: Australian
    Vacation
Sniffles, Sneezes, Hiccups, and
    Coughs
LEGO: Castle Under Attack
LEGO: Rocket Rescue
Star Wars: Journey Through Space
MLB: A Batboy's Day
MLB: Let's Go to the Ballpark!
¡Insectos! *en español*
¡Bomberos! *en español*
Ice Skating Stars
Spider-Man's Worst Enemies
Meet the X-Men
Let's Go Riding

A Note to Parents

DK READERS is a compelling program for beginning readers, designed in conjunction with leading literacy experts, including Dr. Linda Gambrell, Professor of Education at Clemson University. Dr. Gambrell has served as President of the National Reading Conference, College Reading Association, and has recently been elected to serve as President of the International Reading Association.

Beautiful illustrations and superb full-color photographs combine with engaging, easy-to-read stories to offer a fresh approach to each subject in the series. Each DK READER is guaranteed to capture a child's interest while developing his or her reading skills, general knowledge, and love of reading.

The five levels of DK READERS are aimed at different reading abilities, enabling you to choose the books that are exactly right for your child:

Pre-level 1: Learning to read
Level 1: Beginning to read
Level 2: Beginning to read alone
Level 3: Reading alone
Level 4: Proficient readers

The "normal" age at which a child begins to read can be anywhere from three to eight years old, so these levels are only a general guideline.

No matter which level you select, you can be sure that you are helping your child learn to read, then read to learn!

LONDON, NEW YORK, MUNICH,
MELBOURNE, and DELHI

Series Editor Penny Smith
Art Editor Leah Germann
U.S. Editors Elizabeth Hester, John Searcy
DTP Designer Almudena Díaz
Production Angela Graef
Picture Research Myriam Megharbi
Dinosaur Consultant Dougal Dixon

Reading Consultant
Linda Gambrell, Ph.D.

First American Edition, 2006
06 07 08 09 10 10 9 8 7 6 5 4 3 2 1
Published in the United States by DK Publishing, Inc.
375 Hudson Street, New York, New York 10014

DK books are available at special discounts for bulk purchases for sale promotions,
premiums, fundraising, or educational use. For details, contact:
DK Publishing Special Markets
375 Hudson Street
New York, NY 10014
SpecialSales@dk.com

Library of Congress Cataloging-in-Publication Data
Meet the dinosaurs.-- 1st American ed.
p. cm. -- (DK readers. Pre-level 1, Learning to read)
ISBN-13 978-0-7566-1910-7 ISBN-10 0-7566-1910-6 (Paperback)
ISBN-13 978-0-7566-1911-4 ISBN-10 0-7566-1911-4 (Hardcover)
1. Dinosaurs--Juvenile literature. I. Series: Dorling Kindersley readers. Pre-level 1,
Learning to read.
QE861.5.M437 2006
567.9--dc22

2005032704

Color reproduction by Colourscan, Singapore
Printed and bound in China by L Rex Printing Co., Ltd.

The publisher would like to thank the following for their kind permission
to reproduce their photographs:
a=above; c=center; b=below; l=left; r=right; t=top; b/g=background

Alamy Images: Robert Harding Picture Library Ltd 20-21 b/g, 31cr b/g. **Corbis:** Matt
Brown 26-27 b/g; Larry Lee Photography 18-19 b/g, 30cl b/g; W. Wayne Lockwood, MD
4-5c b/g, 8-9 b/g; Charles Mauzy 5tcl b/g, 24-25 b/g; Craig Tuttle 4br b/g, 14-15 b/g, 16-
17 b/g, 28-29 b/g, 31bcl b/g; Jim Zuckerman 6-7, 30cb b/g. **DK Images:** Jon Hughes 4-5c,
8-9. **Getty Images:** J.P. Nacivet 22-23 b/g, 31tr b/g; James Randklev 4c b/g, 10-11 b/g.

All other images © Dorling Kindersley
For more information see: www.dkimages.com

Discover more at
www.dk.com

DK READERS

LEARNING pre-level **1** TO READ

Meet the Dinosaurs

DK
DK Publishing, Inc.

Watch out!
Here come
the dinosaurs.

5

Here is the scary Tyrannosaurus [tuh-RAN-oh-SORE-us]. It has sharp teeth.

Tyrannosaurus

teeth

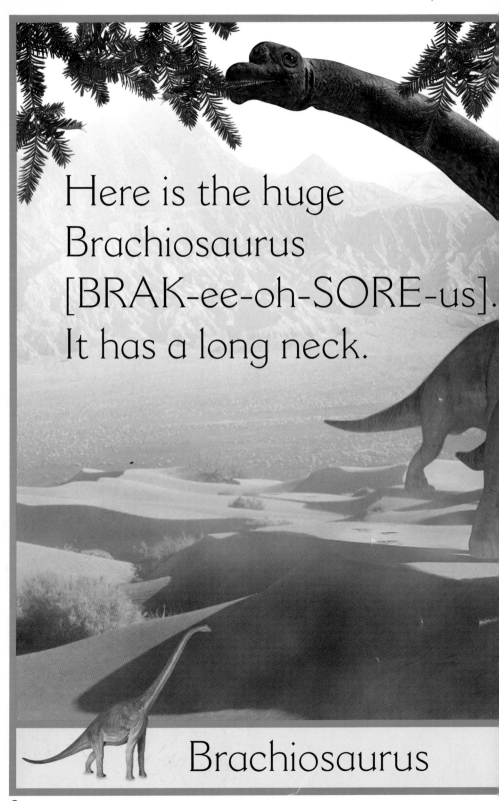

Here is the huge
Brachiosaurus
[BRAK-ee-oh-SORE-us].
It has a long neck.

Brachiosaurus

neck

Here is the tough
Triceratops
[try-SAIR-uh-tops].
It has three horns.

Triceratops

horn

Here is the fierce
Velociraptor
[vuh-LOSS-uh-rap-ter].
It has sharp claws.

Velociraptor

claw

crest

Corythosaurus

Here is the noisy
Corythosaurus
[ko-RITH-oh-SORE-us].
It has a bright crest.

Here is the small
Compsognathus
[KOMP-sug-NAY-thus].
It runs fast.

foot

Compsognathus

Here is the clever
Troodon
[TRO-oh-don].
It has large eyes.

Troodon

eye

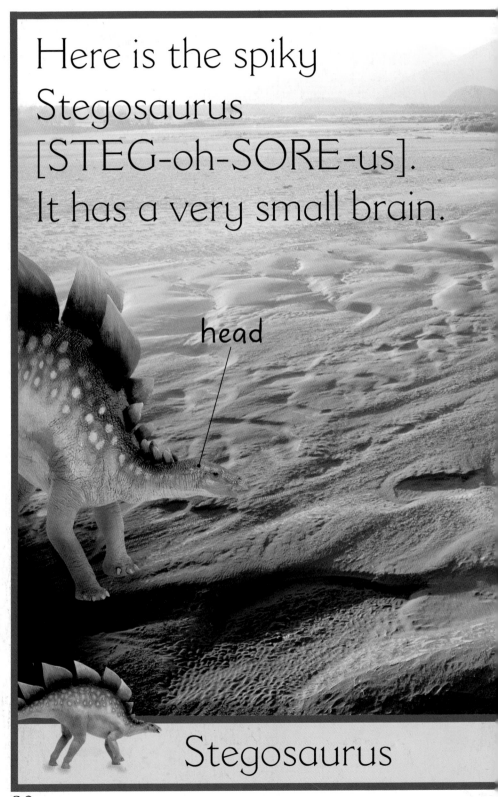

Here is the spiky
Stegosaurus
[STEG-oh-SORE-us].
It has a very small brain.

head

Stegosaurus

Here is the
bird-like Gallimimus
[GAL-uh-MIME-us].
It has thin legs
and a beak.

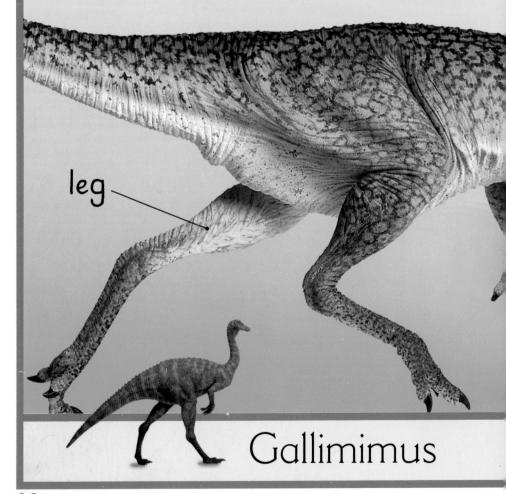

leg

Gallimimus

beak

spike

Iguanodon

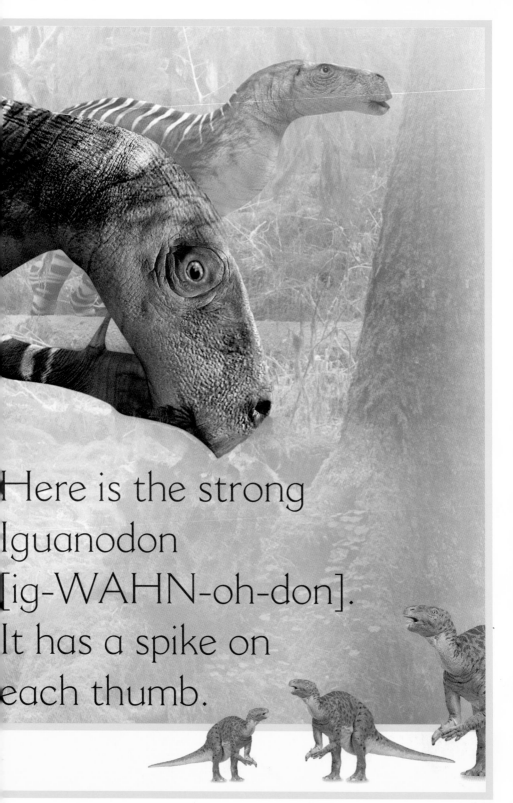

Here is the strong
Iguanodon
[ig-WAHN-oh-don].
It has a spike on
each thumb.

Here is the plant-eater,
Stegoceras
[ste-GOSS-er-us].
It has a thick skull.

skull

Stegoceras

Here is the armored Ankylosaurus [ANG-kuh-low-SORE-us]. It has a tail club.

Ankylosaurus

club

Which dinosaur
do you like best?
The one who is…

clever?

scary?

bird-like?

spiky?

noisy?

31

Picture word list

Tyrannosaurus
page 6

Brachiosaurus
page 8

Triceratops
page 10

Velociraptor
page 12

Corythosaurus
page 14

Compsognathus
page 16

Troodon
page 18

Stegosaurus
page 20

Gallimimus
page 22

Iguanodon
page 24

Stegoceras
page 26

Ankylosaurus
page 28